Flying Geese
Quilt in a Day

Eleanor Burns

To my sister, Judy – whose kindness soars

First printing Feb., 2001

Published by Quilt in a Day®, Inc.
1955 Diamond St, San Marcos, CA 92069

ISBN 1-891776-05-3

Art Director Merritt Voigtlander

Contents

Introduction

Eleanor Burns with Amber's quilt

On a warm clear week-end in December, five young girls joined friend Teresa Varnes and me at my log home in Julian, California, for a weekend of Geese making. Eleven-year-olds Amber Varnes and Leanne Stennett and twelve year old Mary Cecil had already made their first quilts, and were looking forward to new techniques. Anxious thirteen-year-olds Melissa Varnes and Megan Berwick had never finished a quilt!

Amber and Megan selected fabrics in beautiful *Mr. B's Brights*, manufactured by Benartex. Melissa and Leanne went for softer *Fairy Flowers*, another line manufactured by Benartex. Mary's quilt was a combination of the brightest fabrics she could find, including her favorite green!

We started marking and sewing squares on Friday night. Just like a flock of Geese, we flew in the same direction, traveling on the strength of each other! After a hearty breakfast served up by Mike Varnes on Saturday morning, we squared up our patches with the Flying Geese ruler and sewed them into vertical rows. Like Geese, as each girl finished a major part of her quilt, we "honked" words of encouragement. By Saturday afternoon, we were quilting and binding!

Sunday morning was my favorite time as the girls braided each other's hair with colorful scraps from their quilts. One by one, they finished their quilt, machine decorated their labels with embroidery stitches, and made their Pillow Case. Five very proud girls had the sense of Geese to "fly" together!

What a fun weekend! Teresa and I are still honking!

Mary   Megan   Melissa   Amber   Leanne

Amber and Melissa

Mary   Megan   Melissa   Teresa   Amber   El   Leanne

HISTORY

The Flying Geese pattern, also known as Birds in Flight, dates back hundreds of years! Creative women translated the majestic flight of geese into this traditional pattern representing their own flight – from poverty, slavery, or oppression, to a new home and freedom.

When 250,000 pioneers migrated to the west coast in the mid-1800's, they often toted a Flying Geese quilt with them. As a flock of geese flying in formation, pioneers learned they could get there quicker and easier if they traveled together on the strength of each other.

The Underground Railroad is the symbolic term given to the routes enslaved black Americans took to gain their freedom as they traveled, often as far as Canada and Mexico. Free blacks, whites, native Americans and former slaves acted as conductors by aiding fugitive slaves to their freedom. Often, the enslaved people journeyed on their own, braving dangers of every kind. To find their way in unknown territory, slaves were to take their direction, timing, and behavior from the migrating geese. As the geese, runaways were to travel north in the spring. Honking geese would lead them to waterways along their journey so they could rest and eat. Persons assisting runaways could secretly direct them toward freedom just by the way a Flying Geese quilt was hung on the clothesline or backyard fence.

Fabric and Color Selection

The Flying Geese is a traditional quilt featuring vertical rows of rectangular Geese blocks separated by strips called Lattice.

Lattice

A traditional Lattice choice is a stripe which runs the length of the yardage. Overall print yardage can also be used.

Stripe fabrics vary from one design repeated several times to several designs repeated only two or three times. To know what to look for in a stripe, check your quilt size to know how many stripes are required. Identical strips can be used throughout the quilt, or they can be divided into "inside" and "outside" Lattice. The "inside" Lattice are those strips between the vertical Geese, and the "outside" Lattice are the four strips at the sides, top, and bottom.

Finished sizes of quilts are based on stripes that finish at 2½" to 4".

The required amount of stripe yardage is listed in each yardage chart. If your selected stripe does not have enough repeats across, double the amount of stripe yardage to get the needed number of "inside" and "outside" Lattice for your size quilt.

Overall Print fabric can also be purchased, cut selvage to selvage, and seamed together into lengths the same as the Geese.

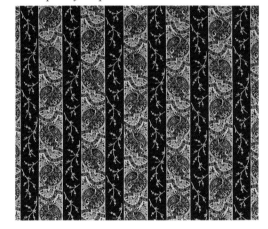

#640 paisley stripe

The width of the stripe depends on the fabric, varying from 3" to 4½" wide. Adjustments can be made in your Borders to get the size quilt you want.

#641 chintz

Featured fabric is from the reproduction 1855 – 1870 civil war era line designed by Nancy Kirk for Benartex, Inc.

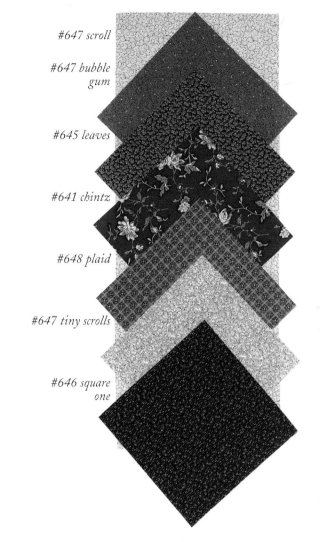

#647 scroll

#647 bubble gum

#645 leaves

#641 chintz

#648 plaid

#647 tiny scrolls

#646 square one

Sky Fabric

The Sky fabric surrounds the Geese. Choose this fabric by laying "inside" Lattice stripes against possible Sky fabrics until you find one with the desired contrast.

The same Sky fabric can be used throughout the quilt, with total yardage given on each quilt size. Sky can also be Scrappy, from multiples of 11" squares. Each size quilt lists how many 11" squares to cut.

Geese Fabrics

Select colors for Geese that coordinate together and with the Lattice stripes, and contrast with the Sky. For planned Geese, select four different fabrics for the Crib Quilt and six different fabrics for larger Quilts. Yardage is given with each size quilt.

For Scrappy Geese, cut coordinated scraps 9½" square from your stash. With this technique, Geese are sewn in multiples of four. Each quilt size lists how many 9½" squares to cut.

Borders, Backing, and Binding

Border fabrics may be any of the Geese fabrics that look attractive beside each other. It's wise to vary the scale of the prints. A good choice for the Binding is the same fabric as the last Border. Choose Backing fabric based on the color of thread you plan to use in the bobbin when machine quilting.

Paste-Up Sheet

Cut small swatches from your fabrics and paste them in place with a glue stick to visualize how finished Geese will look.

Planned

Cut from the selvage edge of fabrics:
(1) 2" square from each Goose fabric
(6) 1½" squares Sky fabric

Cut squares on one diagonal and paste in sequence that appeals to you. When sequence repeats, the top Goose will be next to the bottom Goose.

Scrappy

Make several photocopies of this page for experimentation. Cut 1½" Sky and 2" Geese squares from scraps, cut on one diagonal, and paste in sequence that appeals to you.

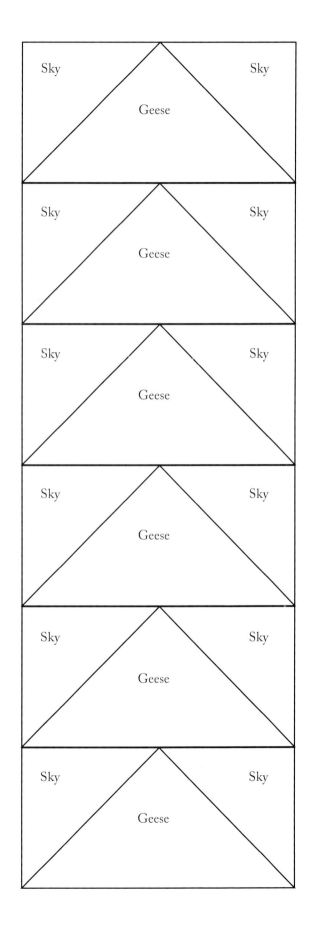

Supplies

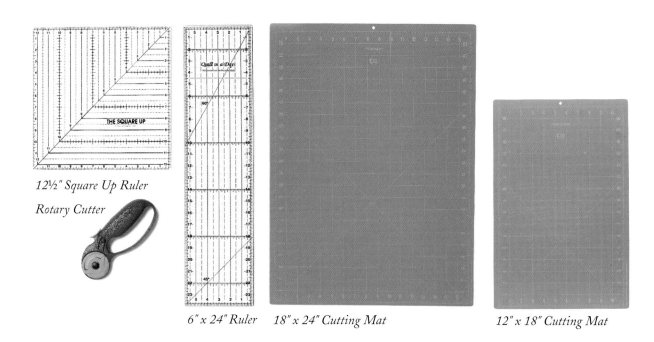

12½" Square Up Ruler

Rotary Cutter

6" x 24" Ruler   *18" x 24" Cutting Mat*   *12" x 18" Cutting Mat*

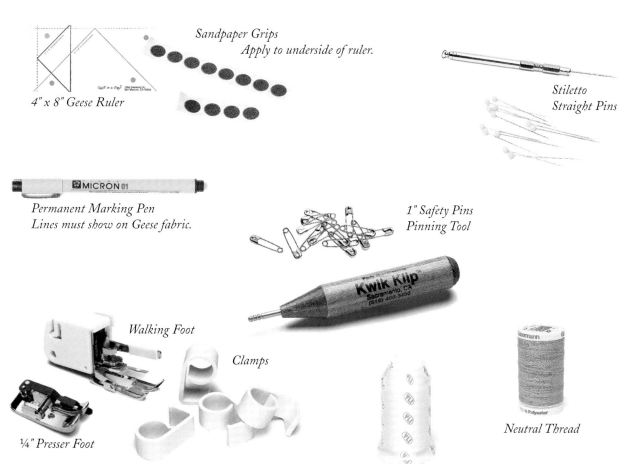

4" x 8" Geese Ruler

Sandpaper Grips
Apply to underside of ruler.

Stiletto
Straight Pins

Permanent Marking Pen
Lines must show on Geese fabric.

1" Safety Pins
Pinning Tool

Walking Foot

Clamps

¼" Presser Foot

Invisible Thread

Neutral Thread

Yardage Charts

Crib

30 Geese
Three rows with ten Geese

Eleanor Burns selected childlike bright polka dots in pinks, blues, and yellows, and a tiny green check for her four Geese. Set against a crisp white Sky and Lattice, the fresh-looking quilt is perfect for a baby boy or girl!

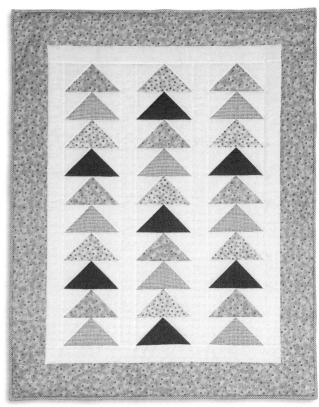

Eleanor Burns   *41" x 53"*

Sky	**1 yd**	
	(3) 11" strips cut into	
	(8) 11" squares	
Geese	**(4) ⅓ yd pieces**	
	cut from each piece	
	(1) 9½" strip cut into	
	(2) 9½" squares	
Lattice (Choose One)		
Stripe	1¼ yds	
	cut lengthwise	
	(2) 3" inside lattice strips	
or	(4) 3" outside lattice strips	
Overall Print	⅔ yd	
	(6) 3" strips	

Borders		
First Border	**1 yd**	
	(5) 5" strips	
Finishing		
Binding	⅔ yd	
	(5) 3" strips	
Backing	1¾ yds	
Batting	48" x 60"	

Lap

36 Geese
Three rows with twelve Geese

Patricia Knoechel selected sky blue and soft yellow pastels for beautiful summertime Geese! For interest, Pat valued the scales of the yellow prints. Flying Geese are separated with 2½" Anniversary Florals vines designed by Eleanor Burns for Benartex.

Patricia Knoechel   *48" x 67"*

Sky	**1½ yds**	
	(4) 11" strips cut into	
	(12) 11" squares	
Geese	**(6) ⅓ yd pieces**	
	cut from each piece	
	(1) 9½" strip cut into	
	(2) 9½" squares	

Lattice (Choose One)

Stripe	**1½ yds**	
	cut lengthwise	
	(2) 3" inside lattice strips	
or	(4) 3" outside lattice strips	
Overall Print	**1 yd**	
	(8) 3" strips	

Borders

First Border	**½ yds**	
	(5) 2¼" strips	
Second Border	**1 yd**	
	(6) 5" strips	

Finishing

Binding	**⅔ yd**	
	(7) 3" strips	
Backing	**3 yds**	
Batting	**54" x 72"**	

Twin

72 Geese
Four rows with eighteen Geese

Amber Varnes selected six bright small scale prints reproduced from 1930's feed sacks. A crisp white tone on tone Lattice sets the Geese into flight. Carol Selepec honked over Amber's precision piecing! Carol expertly added ¼" quilting inside each Geese, and heavy stippling in Sky and Lattice.

Amber Varnes
Quilted by Carol Selepec

Two Borders 62" x 93"
Three Borders 70" x 100"

Sky	**2 yds**	
	(6) 11" strips cut into	
	(18) 11" squares	
Geese	**(6) ⅓ yd pieces**	
	cut from each piece	
	(1) 9½" strip cut into	
	(3) 9½" squares	

Lattice (Choose One)

Stripe	**2¼ yds**	
	cut lengthwise	
	(4) 3"– 4½" inside lattice strips	
or	(4) 3"– 4½" outside lattice strips	
Overall Print	**1¼ yds**	
	(13) 3" strips	

Borders

First Border	**1 yd**	
	(7) 4" strips	
Second Border	**1⅔ yds**	
	(8) 6½" strips	
Third Border	**1½ yds**	
	(9) 5" strips	

Finishing

Binding	**1 yd**	
	(9) 3" strips	
Backing	**6 yds**	
Batting	74" x 104"	

Sales Receipt

Transaction #:   21323
Account #:   00
Date: 15/01/2014   Time: 10:50:09
Cashier: 1   Register #: 1

Item	Description	Amount
		dk -1st
		border
4507103	AIKO GARDEN WINE FLOWER	£13.75
MJ1365416	JOSEPHINE	£20.93
	1.5 @ £13.95	
		moda -2nd
		border
30402	ESS TINY FLOWER WHITE O	£29.97
	3 @ £9.99	*creen*
F52801	RED ALL OVER POPPIES *pink*	£3.06
	0.3 @ £10.20	
2800RC	SPRAYTIME CHRISTMAS RED.	£2.85
	0.3 @ £9.50	*plain*
4265R	ITSY BITS CC RED	£3.23
	0.3 @ £10.75 *wee flower*	
084803	KENSINGTON RED *pasley*	£3.96
	0.3 @ £13.20	
H4182	SAFETY PINS CURVED 38M	£7.00
	2 @ £3.50	

Sub Total	£70.63
Sales Tax	£14.12
Total	£84.75
Cr Card-Visa Tendered	£84.75
Change Due	£0.00

Teresa Varnes
Quilted by Carol Selepec

Double 74" x 92"
Queen 90" x 108"

…ito
…s

…lattice strips
…e lattice strips

Overall Print **2¼ yds**
(16) 3"– 4½" strips

Borders

First Border	**1⅓ yds**
	(8) 5" strips
Second Border	**¾ yd**
	(8) 3" strips
Third Border (Queen only)	**2½ yds**
	(10) 8½" strips

Finishing

Binding		**1 yd**
		(10) 3" strips
Backing		**9½ yds**
Batting	(Double)	**80" x 100"**
	(Queen)	**96" x 114"**

13

King

120 Geese
Six rows with twenty Geese

Sue Bouchard first selected her stripe, a striking purple with multicolor flowers and vines. With "cheer and sunshine" in mind, Sue pulled six bright Geese fabrics from the stripe. Sandy Thompson enhanced the Geese with her creative "free as a bird" stitching. See detail of her beautiful machine quilting on page 37.

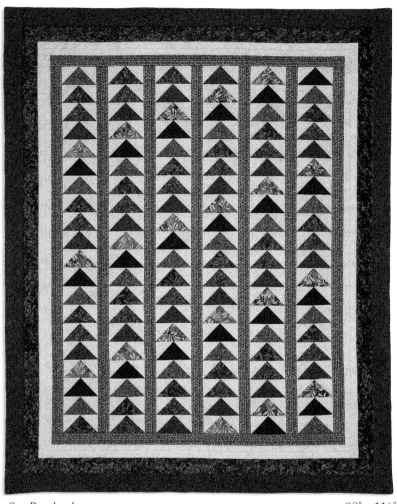

Sue Bouchard
Quilted by Sandy Thompson

98" x 116"

Sky	**3⅓ yds**	**Borders**	
	(10) 11" strips cut into	First Border	**1½ yds**
	(30) 11" squares		(10) 5" strips
Geese	**(6) ⅔ yd pieces**	Second Border	**1 yd**
	cut from each piece		(10) 3" strips
	(2) 9½" strips cut into	Third Border	**2½ yds**
	(5) 9½" squares		(10) 8½" strips
Lattice (Choose One)		**Finishing**	
Stripe	**2¾ yds**	Binding	**1¼ yd**
	cut lengthwise		(12) 3" strips
	(5) 3"– 4½" inside lattice strips		
or	(4) 3"– 4½" outside lattice strips	Backing	**10 yds**
Overall Print	**2½ yds**	Batting	**120" x 120"**
	(18) 3"– 4½" strips		

Pillow Case

12 Geese
Two rows with six Geese

Perfect for left-over Geese, or "from scratch" Geese, the Pillow Case is a welcome accompaniment for all sizes of quilts.

20" x 30"
Teresa Varnes

One Pillow Case

Sky   ⅔ yd

     (2) 11" strips cut into
     (6) 11" squares

Geese   (6) ⅓ yd pieces

     cut from each piece
     (1) 9½" square

Lattice (Choose One)

     Stripe   ¾ yd
            cut lengthwise
     or   (3) 2" strips

     Overall Print   ¼ yd
            (3) 2" strips

Folded Border   ⅛ yd
     (1) 3" strip

Border   ½ yd
     (1) 14" strip

Backing   ¾ yd

Two Pillow Cases

Sky   ⅔ yd

     (2) 11" strips cut into
     (6) 11" squares

Geese   (6) ⅓ yd pieces

     cut from each piece
     (1) 9½" square

Lattice (Choose One)

     Stripe   ¾ yd
            cut lengthwise
     or   (6) 3" strips

     Overall Print   ½ yd
            (6) 2" strips

Folded Border   ¼ yd
     (2) 3" strips

Border   1 yd
     (2) 14" strips

Backing   1½ yds

Cutting Squares

Cutting 11" Sky Squares

*Yardage charts are based on getting three 11"
squares from one 11" strip. If you have a 45" wide
piece of fabric, and can cut four 11" squares from
one strip, you can cut less strips.*

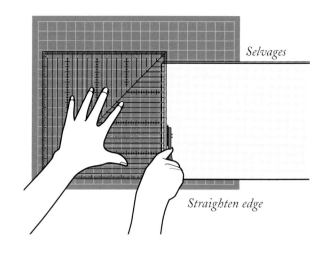

Selvages

Straighten edge

1. Cut a nick in one selvage, the tightly woven
   edge on both sides of the fabric. Tear across
   the grain from selvage to selvage.

2. Press fabric, particularly the torn edge.

3. Fold fabric in half, matching the frayed
   edges. Don't worry about the selvages lining
   up correctly as this is not always possible.
   Fold again.

4. Lay fabric on cutting mat with most of it to
   the right. Make sure all four layers of the
   torn edge are lined up at the left edge. Lay
   the ¼" line on 12½" Square Up ruler along
   the torn edge, and trim for a clean straight
   edge.

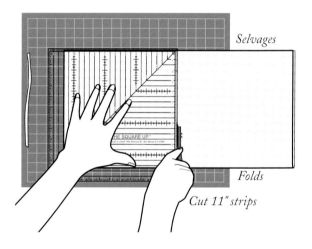

Selvages

Folds

Cut 11" strips

5. Reposition ruler, and line up 11" line on cut
   edge. Cut an 11" strip.

6. Open strip once so strip is approximately
   21" wide.

7. Square off selvage edges. Layer cut two
   11" squares.

8. Open remaining part of strip. Cut one
   11" square.

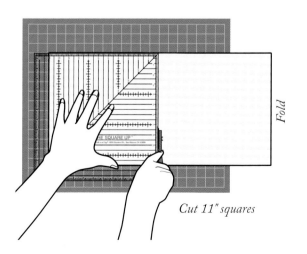

Fold

Cut 11" squares

9. Repeat until you have the desired number
   of 11" Sky squares.

Cutting 9½" Geese Squares

Yardage charts are based on cutting four 9½" squares from one 9½" strip.

1. Repeating previous steps, fold fabric in fourths, and cut 9½" strips.

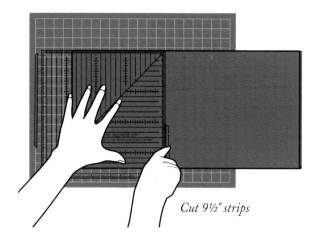

Cut 9½" strips

2. Open strip once, and square off selvage edges. Layer cut four 9½" squares.

3. Repeat until you have the desired number of 9½" squares from each set of Geese fabric.

    One 11" Sky square and one 9½" Geese square makes four Geese. Cut this many squares:

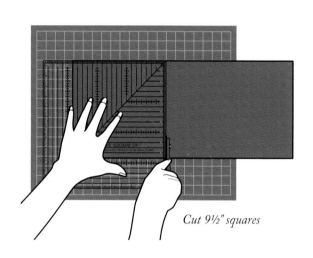

Cut 9½" squares

Planned

	11" Sky	9½" Geese Fabric
Crib	8	2 each from 4 fabrics
Lap	12	2 each from 6 fabrics
Twin	18	3 each from 6 fabrics
Dbl/Queen	24	4 each from 6 fabrics
King	30	5 each from 6 fabrics

Scrappy

	11" Sky	9½" Geese Fabric
Crib	8	8
Lap	12	12
Twin	18	18
Dbl/Queen	24	24
King	30	30

Making 4" x 8" Flying Geese

1. Place 9½" Geese square right sides together and centered on 11" Sky square. Press.

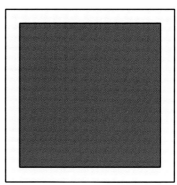

Each set makes four Geese.

2. Place 6" x 24" ruler on squares so ruler touches all four corners. Draw diagonal line across squares with marking pen.

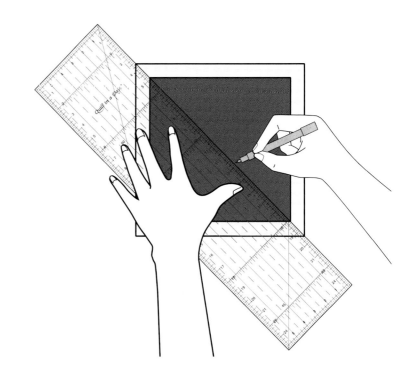

3. Pin.

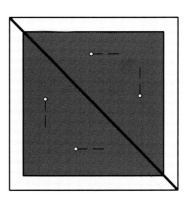

4. Sew **exactly** ¼" from drawn line. Use 15 stitches per inch or 2.0 on computerized machines. Assembly-line sew several squares.

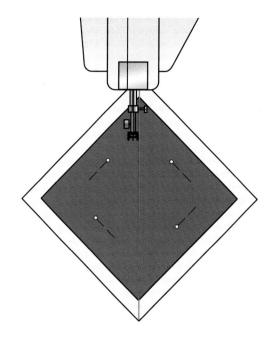

5. Turn and sew ¼" seam from second side of drawn line. Press to set seam.

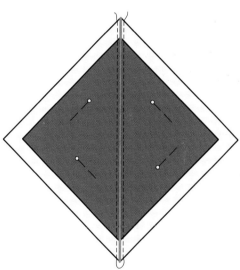

Turn and sew second side.

6. Remove pins. Cut on drawn line.

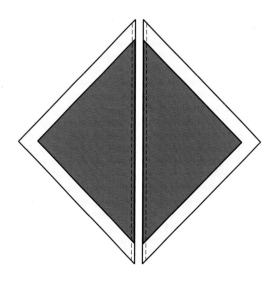

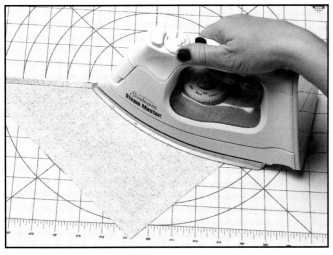

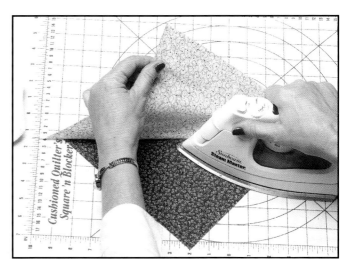

7. Place on pressing mat with **large triangle on top. Press to set seam.**

8. Open and press flat. Check that there are no tucks, and **seam is pressed toward larger triangle.**

9. Place pieces right sides together so that opposite fabrics touch with Geese matched to Sky. **Seams are parallel with each other.**

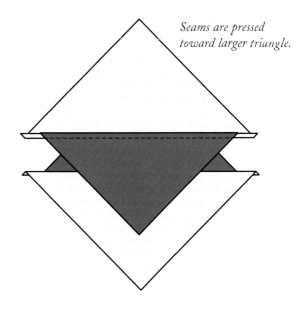

Seams are pressed toward larger triangle.

10. Match up outside edges. Notice that there is a gap between seams. **The seams do not lock.**

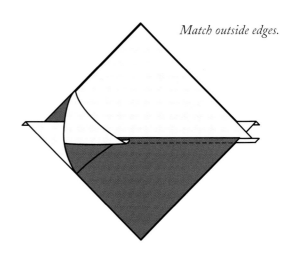

Match outside edges.

11. Draw a diagonal line across seams. Pin.

12. Sew ¼" from both sides of drawn line. Hold seam flat with stiletto. Press to set seam.

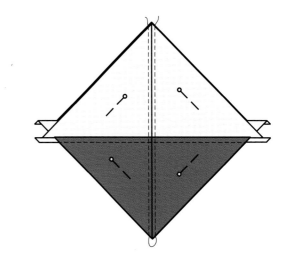

13. Cut on the drawn line.

14. Clip the seam allowance to the vertical seam midway between the horizontal seams. This allows the seam allowance to be pressed away from Geese.

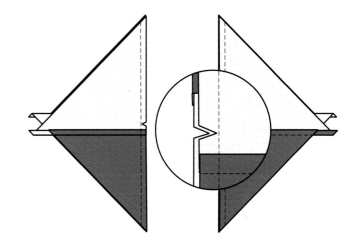

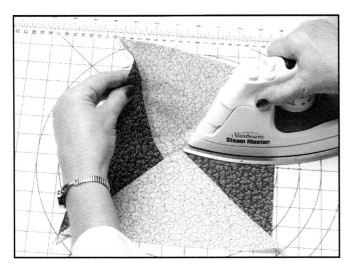

15. From right side, press into Geese seams. Press each half open.

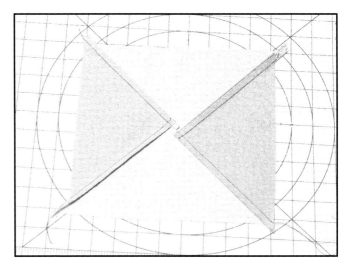

16. At clipped seam, fabric is pressed away from Geese.

Squaring Up With Geese Ruler

1. Place Geese on small cutting mat so you can rotate mat as you cut.

2. Line up ruler's green lines on 45º sewn lines. Line up dotted line with peak of triangle for the ¼" seam allowance.

3. Cut block in half to separate the two patches.

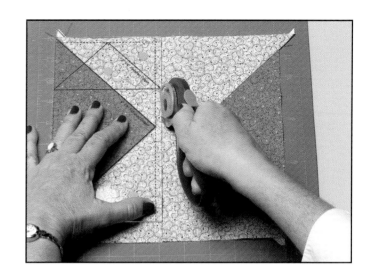

4. Trim off excess fabric on all four sides, turning mat as you cut. Hold ruler securely on fabric so it will not shift while cutting.

5. Repeat with all Geese. Patch should measure 4½" x 8½".

Total Number of Geese Needed	
Crib	30
Lap	36
Twin	72
Dbl/Queen	90
King	120

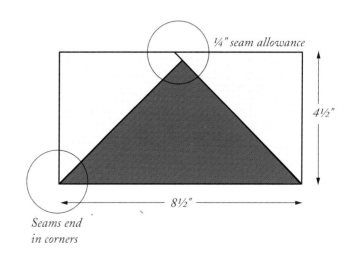

¼" seam allowance

4½"

8½"

Seams end
in corners

Squaring Up Without Geese Ruler

1. With a 6" x 12" ruler, line up the 45º line on a Geese seam, and the ¼" line on the peak.

2. Cut across, keeping an exact ¼" seam allowance beyond peak.

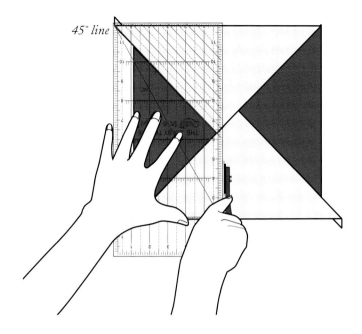

45° line

3. Turn second piece and repeat. A small strip will be cut out of center. Stack. Set the 6" x 12" ruler aside.

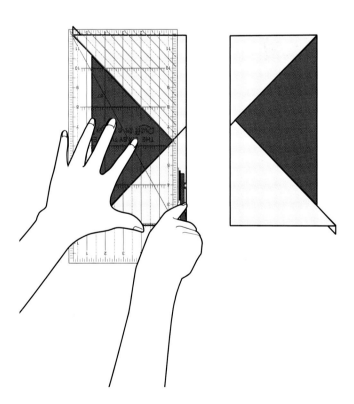

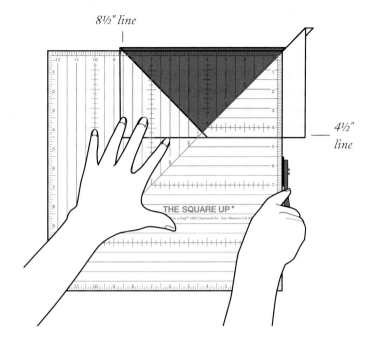

8½" line

4½" line

4. With the 12½" square ruler, place the diagonal line on the seam. Line up the bottom edge of the Geese with the 4½" line on the ruler. Line up the left edge at 8½". Trim right and top edges.

5. Turn Geese patch. **Do not turn ruler.** Line up on 4½" x 8½" lines. Trim on right edge.

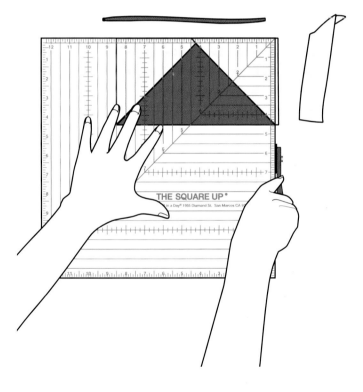

Total Number of Geese Needed	
Crib	30
Lap	36
Twin	72
Dbl/Queen	90
King	120

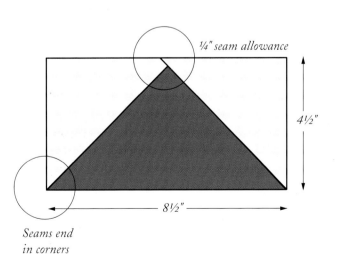

¼" seam allowance

4½"

8½"

Seams end
in corners

Sewing Geese into Rows

Sewing Geese for Crib Quilt

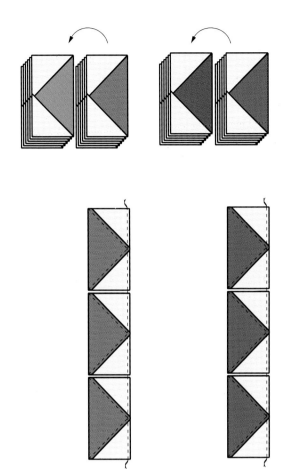

1. Stack Geese in sewing order. Separate into pairs.

2. Flip Goose patch on right to Goose patch on the immediate left. Match outside edges. Hold seam flat with stiletto.

3. Sew accurate ¼" seam, crossing point as you stitch. Check to see that point is "crisp" on right side.

4. Assembly-line sew all pairs. Clip threads.

5. **Set two pairs of each aside.**

6. Assembly-line sew remaining pairs into sets of four.

7. Sew together two sets of four plus one pair. Make two rows the same and one row different. One pair of Geese is left over.

8. Press seams toward point of Geese. Turn to page 29 for finishing.

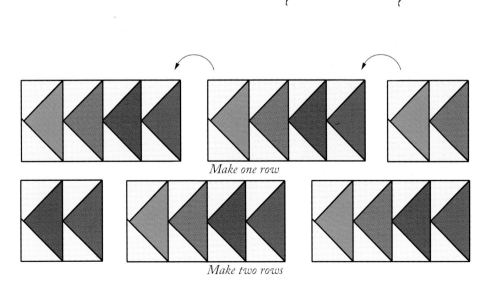

Make one row

Make two rows

Sewing Geese for Larger Quilts

King Only: Set aside two Geese from each color.

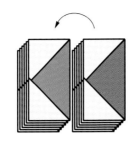 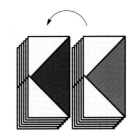 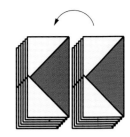

1. Stack Geese in sewing order. Separate into pairs.

2. Flip Goose patch on right to Goose patch on the immediate left. Match outside edges. Hold seam flat with stiletto.

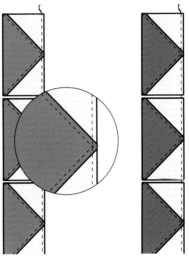 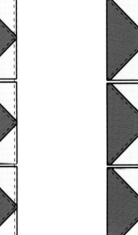

3. Sew accurate ¼" seam, crossing point as you stitch. Check to see that point is "crisp" on right side.

4. Assembly-line sew all pairs. Clip threads.

5. Assembly-line sew all pairs into sets of six. To manage, work with a few at a time.

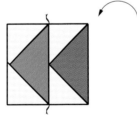  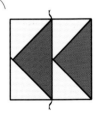

6. Clip connecting threads.

7. Place Geese on pressing mat wrong side up. Press seams away from base of Geese.

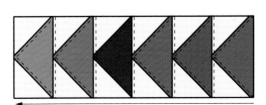

Press seams away from base.

8. Turn over and press from right side. Make sure there are no tucks at seams.

Sewing Vertical Rows of Geese

1. **Lap Robe:** Sew together two sets for twelve Geese in a row. Make three rows.

Lap Robe
2 sets of six
3 rows

2. **Twin Quilt:** Sew together three sets for eighteen Geese in a row. Make four rows.

Twin
3 sets of six
4 rows

3. **Double/Queen Quilt:** Sew together three sets for eighteen Geese in a row. Make five rows.

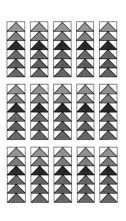

Double/Queen
3 sets of six
5 rows

4. **King Quilt:** Sew together three sets for eighteen Geese in a row. Make six rows.

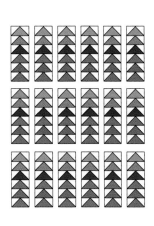

King
3 sets of six
6 rows

5. Lay out the rows next to each other to see how they will appear in the finished quilt.

6. If you don't want all the same Geese fabrics to line up in horizontal rows, vary the formation by "unsewing" one block from the bottom of the second row and sewing it to the top.

7. "Unsew" two from the bottom of the third row and sew to the top. Continue "unsewing" and adding to the top, or plan your own design.

   King Only: Take 12 Geese that were set aside. At the bottom of each row, add two Geese that are in the same order as the top two Geese.

Example of a Double/Queen Quilt

8. From wrong side, press seams upward away from base of Geese.

9. Press from right side, making certain there are no tucks at seams.

Unsewing

Hold rotary cutter between thumb and forefinger in right hand. Place thumb and forefinger of left hand near seam to be "unsewn." Pull tension on fabric with remaining three fingers of right hand. With both hands pulling in opposite directions, pull seam apart, exposing thread. Keeping fingers out of the way, drop rotary blade against stitches and cut thread as you pull. Pick out stitches in seam allowance.

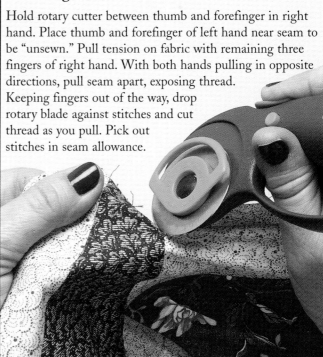

Sewing Top Together

Cutting Striped Lattice

1. Measure length of Geese rows.

2. Lay out stripe fabric. Place 6" x 24" ruler's ¼" line on edge of stripe for seam allowance. Rotary cut one side of stripe the length of fabric.

3. Place ¼" line on opposite side of stripe, and cut.

4. Cut Lattice strips 2" longer than Geese rows.

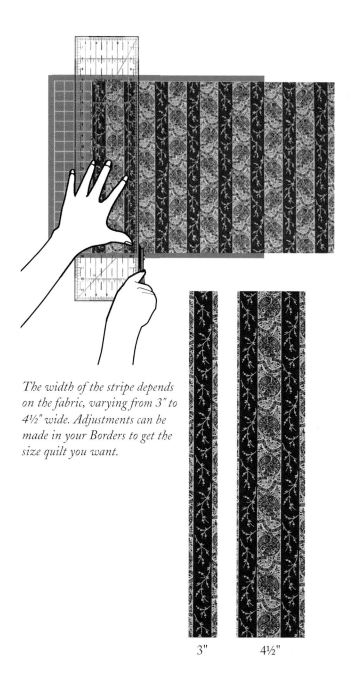

The width of the stripe depends on the fabric, varying from 3" to 4½" wide. Adjustments can be made in your Borders to get the size quilt you want.

3"   4½"

Piecing Overall Print Fabric

1. Square selvage edges.

2. Sew together into one long strip.

3. Cut Lattice strips 2" longer than Geese rows.

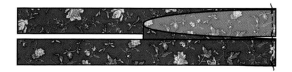

Sewing Lattice to Geese

1. Lay out vertical rows in desired pattern with Geese pointing down.

2. Lay Lattice strips around Geese rows. Place carefully if Lattice strips are directional or if their print requires special placement. Position strips to extend about 1" at each end of Geese rows.

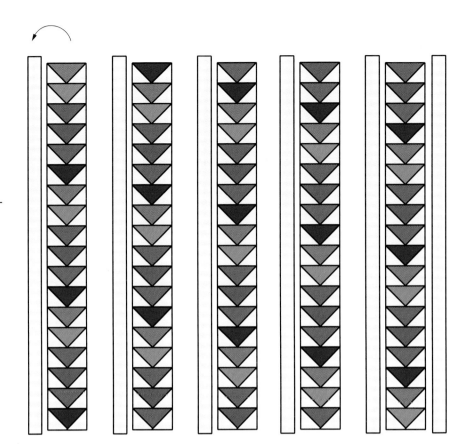

3. Flip Geese to Lattice on left. Lattice should extend an inch at both ends. Pin at each seam.

4. Sew Geese to Lattice with accurate ¼" seam.

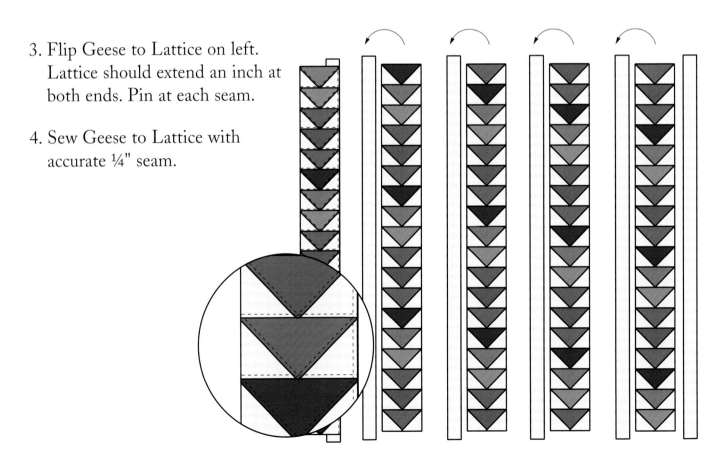

Use stiletto to hold seams flat. Check on right side for "crisp" points.

5. Place strip set on pressing mat with Lattice on top. Set seam, open, and press.

6. Sew Lattice to right side of last vertical row.

7. Trim ends off Lattice.

8. **Optional Marking:** Lay ruler horizontally on first Goose seam. Back ruler off slightly to allow for pencil or fine chalk mark. Mark edge of Lattice **in seam allowance** as a matching point for next Geese strip.

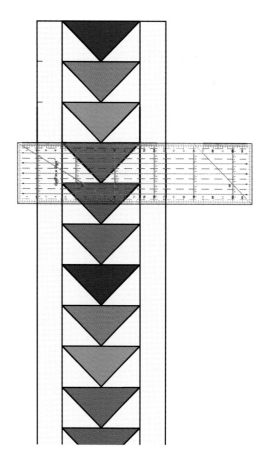

9. Mark each matching point on inside Lattice for every horizontal seam. Replace in layout.

10. Pair, pin, and sew together.

11. Press seam on each pair toward Lattice.

12. Sew rows together into one quilt.

13. Press seams toward Lattice.

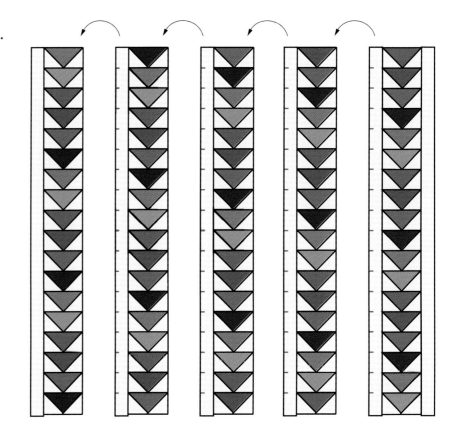

14. Add top and bottom Lattice, trim ends, and press.

15. Put quilt top on your bed. Estimate the finished size with planned Borders. You may desire to change or add more Borders.

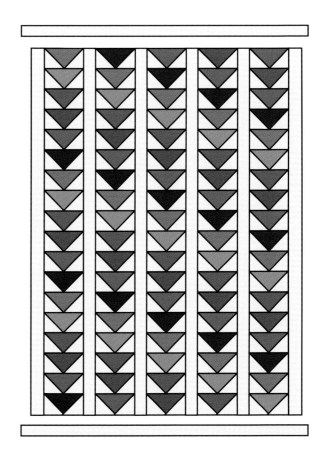

Finishing Your Quilt

Adding Borders

1. Cut Borders to desired sizes. Refer to Yardage Charts, pages 10 to 14.

2. Trim away the selvages at a right angle.

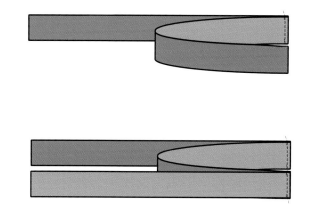

3. Lay the first strip right side up. Lay the second strip right sides to it. Backstitch, stitch and stitch again.

4. Continue assembly-line sewing all the short ends together into long pieces for each fabric.

Sewing Borders to Quilt Top

1. Cut First Border pieces the average length of both sides.

2. Pin and sew to the sides. Fold out and press seams toward Border.

3. Measure the width and cut Border pieces for the top and bottom. Pin and sew. Press seams toward the Border.

4. Repeat with any additional Borders.

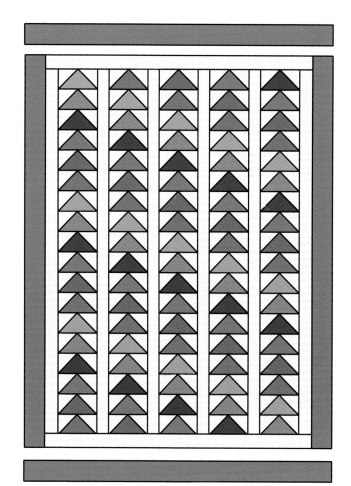

Layering the Quilt

1. Spread out the Backing on a large table or floor area with the right side down. Clamp the fabric to the edge of the table with quilt clips or tape the Backing to the floor. Do not stretch the Backing.

2. Layer the batting on top of the Backing, and pat flat.

3. With the quilt top right side up, center on the Backing. Smooth until all layers are flat. Clamp or tape outside edges.

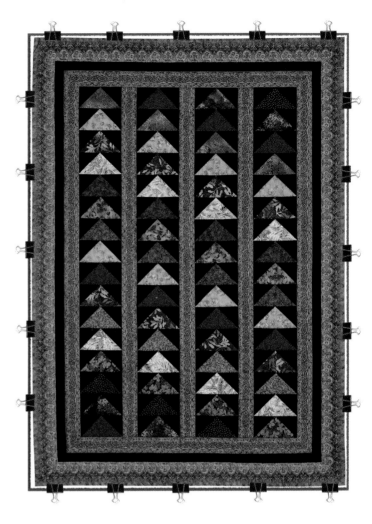

Safety Pinning

1. Use 1" safety pins. Safety pin through all layers in the center of every Geese and center of Lattice every three to five inches.

2. Catch tip of pin in grooves on pinning tool, and close pins.

3. Use pinning tool to open pins when removing them. Store pins opened.

"Stitch in the Ditch" in Lattice and Borders

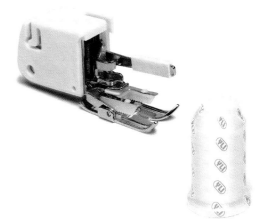

1. Thread your machine with matching thread or invisible thread. If you use invisible thread, loosen your top tension. Match the bobbin thread to the Backing.

2. Attach your walking foot, and lengthen the stitch to 8 to 10 stitches per inch or 3.5 on computerized machines.

3. Roll one side to the center. Clip the rolls in place.

4. Spread the vertical seams open, and "stitch in the ditch."

5. Unroll the quilt to the next vertical seam. Clip the roll in place, and "stitch in the ditch."

6. Continue to unroll and roll the quilt until all the seams are stitched.

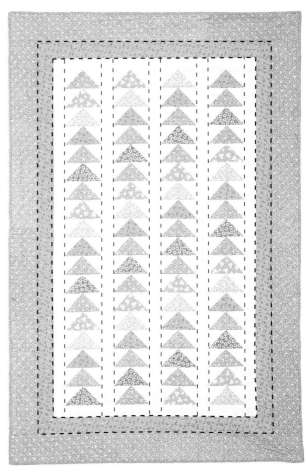

"Stitch in the Ditch" in Lattice and Borders

Quilting Geese

Choose one of the following methods, pages 35 to 37.

1. With walking foot, stitch base of Geese, raise presser foot and skip over Lattice, and begin again on next base. It's best to lock stitch each section so connecting threads do not pull out.

2. Pivot with needle down as you stitch around the points of the Geese. Skip over Lattice each time. Clip connecting threads.

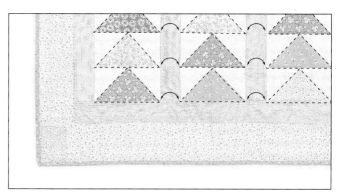

"Stitch in the Ditch" around the Geese

Quilting Geese with Darning Foot

Attach darning foot to sewing machine and drop feed dogs or cover feed dogs with a plate. No stitch length is required as you control the length. Place a fine needle on machine, and a little hole throat plate. Use invisible or regular thread in the top and regular thread to match the Backing in the bobbin. Loosen the top tension if using invisible thread.

Quilt ¼" Inside Geese

1. Place hands flat on sides of one Geese.

2. Bring bobbin thread up ¼" away from seam. Lock stitch and clip thread tails.

3. Free motion stitch around Geese starting at the top, stitching down the right side, across the base, and back up the left side. It's not necessary to turn the quilt as you stitch.

4. Lock stitch and cut threads.

¼" Quilting and Meandering Stippling by Carol Selepec

Oval Stitching in Geese

1. Place hands flat on sides of one Geese.

2. Bring bobbin thread up ¼" away from seam.

3. Lock stitch and clip thread tails.

4. Free motion stitch oval design, starting with a smaller oval on the side, to a larger oval in the center, and ending with a smaller oval.

Stippling Sky

1. Stretch Sky fabric with your fingertips. Move fabric in a steady motion while running machine at a constant speed.

2. Move fabric underneath needle side to side, and forward and backward, making meandering stitches or loops with stitches. Fill in Sky with stitches.

3. Lock off with tiny stitches and clip threads at the end.

Oval Stitching and Loop Stippling by Sandy Thompson

Binding

Use a walking foot attachment and regular thread on top and in the bobbin to match the Binding.

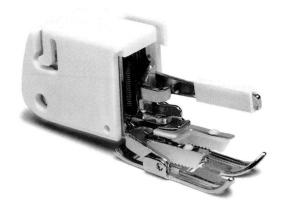

1. Square off the selvage edges, and sew 3" strips together lengthwise.

2. Fold and press in half with wrong sides together.

3. Line up the raw edges of the folded Binding with the raw edges of the quilt in the middle of one side.

4. Begin stitching 4" from the end of the Binding. Sew with 10 stitches per inch, or 3.0 to 3.5 stitch length on computerized machines.

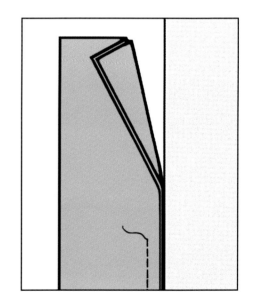

5. At the corner, stop the stitching ¼" from the edge with the needle in the fabric. Raise the presser foot and turn the quilt to the next side. Put the foot back down.

6. Stitch backwards ¼" to the edge of the Binding, raise the foot, and pull the quilt forward slightly.

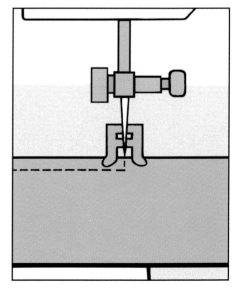

7. Fold the Binding strip straight up on the diagonal. Fingerpress the diagonal fold.

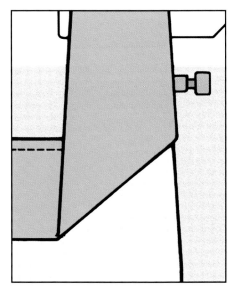

8. Fold the Binding strip straight down with the diagonal fold underneath. Line up the top of the fold with the raw edge of the Binding underneath.

9. Begin sewing from the edge.

10. Continue stitching and mitering the corners around the outside of the quilt.

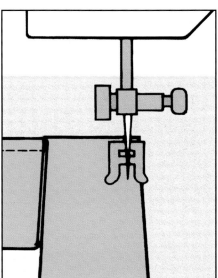

11. Stop stitching 4" from where the ends will overlap.

12. Line up the two ends of Binding. Trim the excess with a ½" overlap.

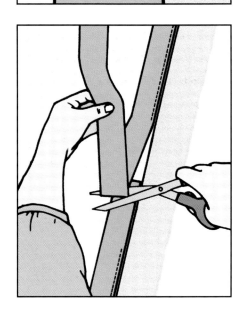

13. Open out the folded ends and pin right sides together. Sew a ¼" seam.

14. Continue to stitch the Binding in place.

15. Trim the batting and Backing up to the raw edges of the Binding.

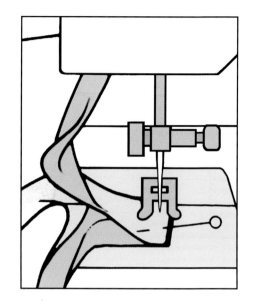

16. Fold the Binding to the back side of the quilt. Pin in place so that the folded edge on the Binding covers the stitching line. Tuck in the excess fabric at each miter on the diagonal.

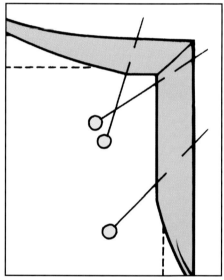

17. From the right side, "stitch in the ditch" using invisible thread on the front side, and a bobbin thread to match the Binding on the back side. Catch the folded edge of the Binding on the back side with the stitching.

    Optional: Hand stitch Binding in place.

18. Sew on an identification label on the Back.

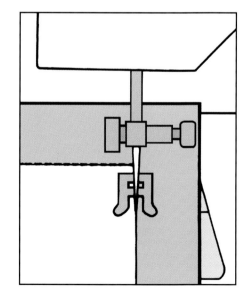

Pillow Case

20" x 30"

You need a total of 12 Geese for one Pillow Case. Use left-overs from your quilt, or make new Geese. Each set of 11" Sky and 9½" Geese squares produces four Geese. With six different fabrics, you make a total of 24 Geese, enough for two Pillow Cases.

Yardage for the Pillow Case is on page 15.

Making Pillow Front

1. Make Geese from each set of six fabrics. Follow directions starting on page 18.

2. Make two rows with six Geese in each row.

3. Press seams away from base of Geese toward point.

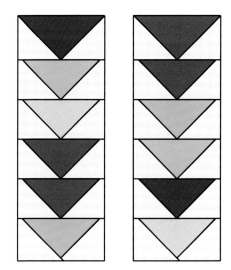

4. Measure length of Geese. Cut three 2" Lattice strips same length.

5. Pin and sew Lattice and Geese together, carefully lining up Geese.

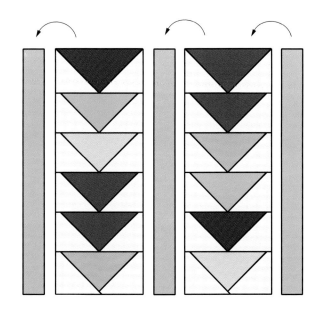

6. Set seams with Lattice on top, open, and press seams toward Lattice.

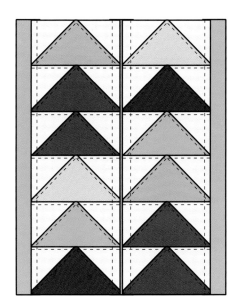

Lining Pillow Case

1. Cut Backing fabric in half on fold.

2. Stack two Backing pieces **right side up**.

3. Place Pillow front **right sides together** to layered Backings.

4. Pin around three sides. Trim Backings to match Pillow front.

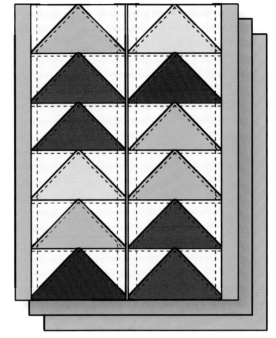

Press seams toward lattice.

5. Backstitch, sew around sides and bottom.

6. Insert hand inside Pillow Case, grasp Pillow front, and turn right side out.

7. Pull out corners with stiletto. Press edges flat.

8. Pull Backings apart. Pin one Backing to Pillow front at open end. This Backing lines the patchwork so seams do not fray with washing and wear.

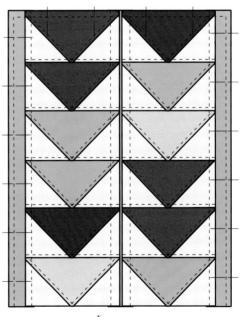

Leave open

Making Borders

1. Press 3" Folded Border in half lengthwise wrong sides together.

2. Match raw edges of Folded Border and 14" Border. Sew with seam slightly less than ¼".

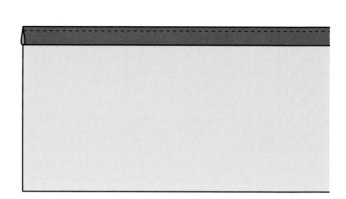

3. Press in half lengthwise, wrong sides together.

4. Open ends. Matching Folded Border, sew short ends together into a "tube." Press seam open.

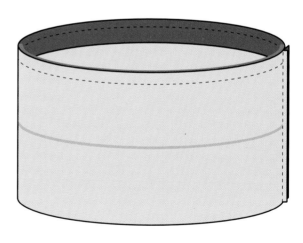

5. Refold "tube" right side out. Folded Border is on inside of "tube". Press.

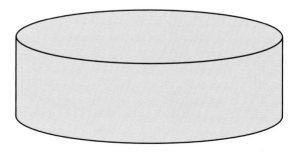

6. Slip "tube" over end of Pillow. Match side seams and raw edges. Pin around circle.

7. Sew with ¼" seam.

8. Zigzag stitch for a clean finished edge.

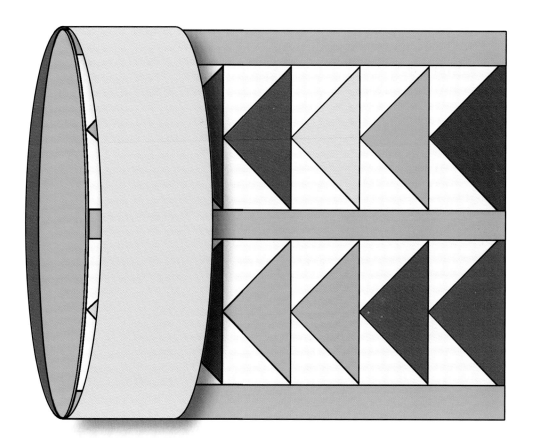

Acknowledgements

Let's flap our wings for these great folks!

Quilters: Sue Bouchard, Lori Forsythe, Patricia Knoechel, Carol Selepec, Sandy Thompson, Amber Varnes, Teresa Varnes

Fabric: Nancy Kirk for an authentic line of reproduction 1855-1870 Civil War Era designs

Selim Benardete for quality Benartex fabrics used in Geese quilts

Index

Order Information

Quilt in a Day books offer a wide range of techniques and are directed toward a variety of skill levels. If you do not have a quilt shop in your area, you may write or call for a complete catalog and current price list of all books and patterns published by Quilt in a Day®, Inc.

Other books that use the Flying Geese Method

Now available from Quilt in a Day – Two different Geese Rulers to make patches in four sizes.

Christmas Quilts and Crafts

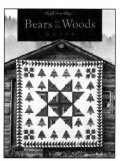
Bears in the Woods

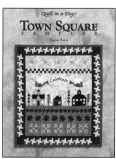
Town Square Sampler

Pioneer Sampler

Stars Across America

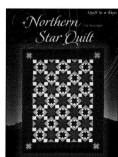
Northern Star Quilt

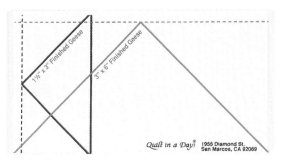
1½" x 3" and 3" x 6" Geese Ruler

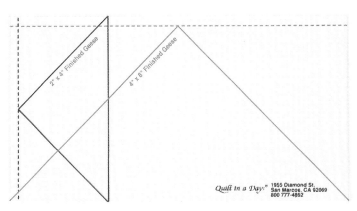
2" x 4" and 4" x 8" Geese Ruler

Quilt in a Day®, Inc. • 1955 Diamond Street, • San Marcos, CA 92069
Toll Free: 1 800 777-4852 • Fax: (760) 591-4424
Internet: www.quiltinaday.com • 8 am to 5 pm Pacific Time

Lori Forsythe selected six vibrant red fabrics, and turned them into a colorful Christmas gift for her sister. The quilt is so bright, its brings cheer all year! Lori is a new quiltmaker, and found the Flying Geese quilt to be fast and fun!

Teresa Varnes used leftover 4" x 8" Geese, and sewed them together with 2" x 4" Geese for a fresh new look. To make your own 2" x 4" Geese, cut 5½" Geese squares, and 7" Sky squares. For every two large Geese, make four small Geese. Follow the instructions on pages 18 to 22, and use the red 2" x 4" lines on your Geese ruler to square them up.

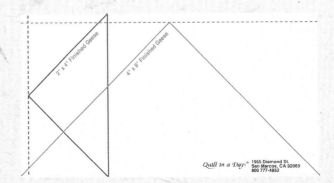

2" x 4" Finished Geese

4" x 8" Finished Geese

Quilt in a Day® 1955 Diamond St.
San Marcos, CA 92069
800 777-4852